MW00904573

NEIL ARMSTRONG

THE FIRST MAN TO WALK ON THE MOON

Biography for Kids 9-12
Children's Biography Books

BABY PROFESSOR
EDUCATION KIDS

Speedy Publishing LLC

40 E. Main St. #1156

Newark, DE 19711

www.speedypublishing.com

Copyright 2017

All Rights reserved. No part of this book may be reproduced or used in any way or form or by any means whether electronic or mechanical, this means that you cannot record or photocopy any material ideas or tips that are provided in this book.

Neil Armstrong was an astronaut who was the first man to walk on the moon. Approximately six hundred million viewers watched on television as he made this memorable walk on July 21, 1969. Read further to learn about Neil Armstrong and how he became to be the first man to walk on the moon.

WHERE WAS HE RAISED?

Neil was born in Wapakoneta, Ohio on August 5, 1930. When his father took him to his first air show, he discovered his love for flying. It was his goal from then on to become a pilot and at the young age of 15, he obtained his pilot's license.

WAPAKONETA OHIO DOWNTOWN

Neil attended Purdue University, earning his bachelor's degree in the field of aerospace engineering. Later, he received his master's degree at the University of Southern California.

He was called up to the Navy while attending college and he became a fighter pilot. He flew fighters from the aircraft carriers as he was fighting in the Korean War. His plane was struck by enemy fire at one point, however he was ejected and safely rescued.

BECOMING AN ASTRONAUT

After he graduated from college, he became a test pilot and flew all types of experimental planes to see how well they performed. While it was an extremely dangerous job, it was quite exciting. During his career, he went on to fly more than 200 types of aircraft.

NEIL ARMSTRONG

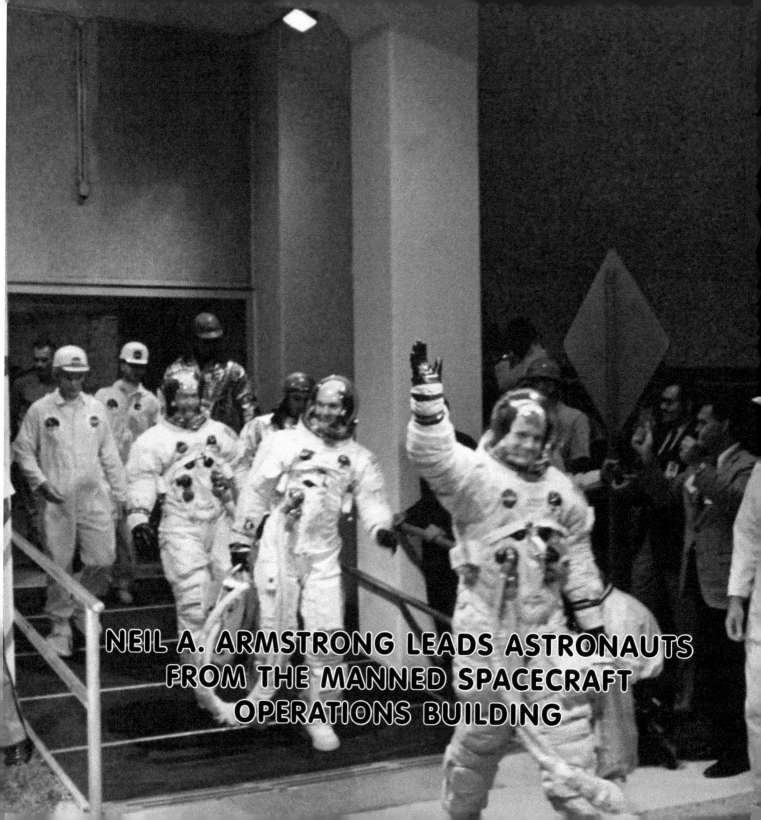

NEIL A. ARMSTRONG LEADS ASTRONAUTS FROM THE MANNED SPACECRAFT OPERATIONS BUILDING

In September of 1962, Armstrong applied with NASA to be an astronaut and was chosen for the NASA Astronaut Corps. After going through a series of physical tests that were quite harsh, he passed and soon was a part the second group of nine NASA astronauts, or what became known as the "new nine".

THE GEMINI 8

His first trip to space was on the Gemini 8. He was assigned as command pilot of the capsule and was the first to successfully pilot the docking of two separate vehicles while in space. However, this mission was cut short once the capsules started to roll.

GEMINI 8 ATLAS-AGENA LAUNCH

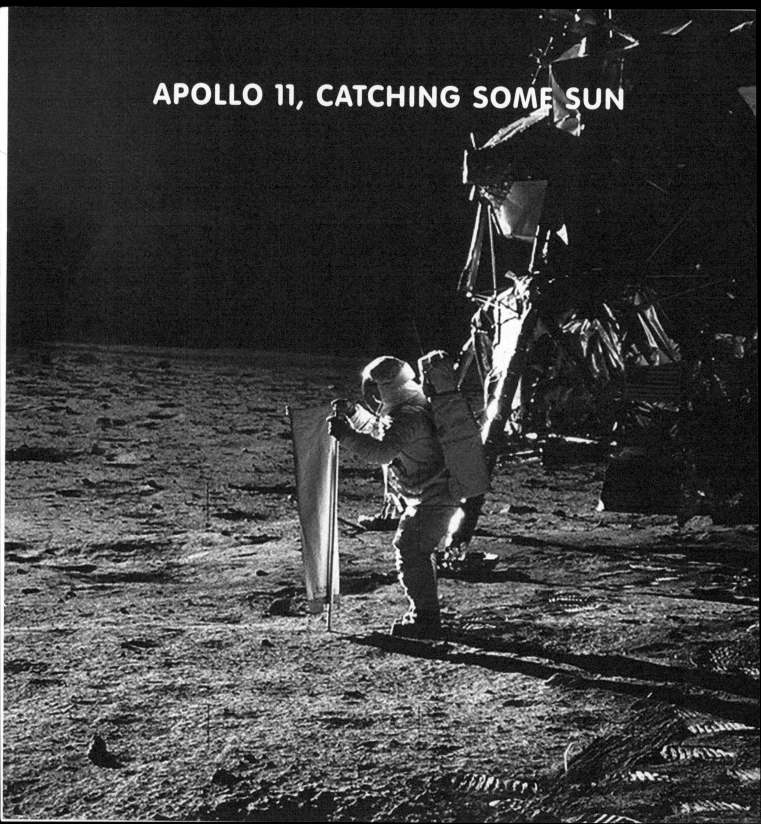

APOLLO 11, CATCHING SOME SUN

APOLLO 11 AND THE WALK ON THE MOON

Armstrong was offered command of Apollo 11 on December 23, 1968, which would be the first landing of a manned spacecraft on the moon and was a very exciting era for the entire country. The United States had been in a race with the Soviet Union to land the first man onto the moon. If this flight was successful, he would be that man.

After several months of preparation and practice, Apollo 11 was launched on July 16, 1969 from Kennedy Space Center which was located in Florida. There was a slight scare during the flight when Neil had to take control manually over the landing. If the landing took too much time, they would be short on fuel. However, the landing was successful, with about 40 seconds of fuel left.

Once they landed on the moon, Armstrong said "Houston, Tranquility Base here. The Eagle has landed". Once they landed, Armstrong was first to leave their craft and walk onto the Moon. July 21, 1969 is that historic date. Upon being the first man on the Moon, his famous words were "That's one small step for man, one giant leap for mankind". During this trip, Buzz Aldrin also walked on it.

They stayed on the Moon for more than 21 hours collecting Moon rocks. As the lunar module, named the Eagle, remained on the Moon, Michael Collins, the third

astronaut, orbited it from the command module. On July 24th, the three pilots arrived safely back to Earth, landing in the Pacific Ocean as heroes.

UNIVERSITY OF CINCINATTI

AFTER APOLLO 11

Armstrong held several positions with NASA after the Apollo 11 flight. Additionally, he worked at the University of Cincinnati as a professor of aerospace engineering.

THE SPACE RACE

The Soviet Union and the United States engaged in a competition during the Cold War, in order to find out who had the greatest technology in space. Included in this competition were events such as who could get the first manned craft into orbit and who would be first to walk on the moon. This race was considered to be important since it revealed to the world which country had the best technology, science and economic system.

UNITED STATES AND SOVIET
UNION SPACE CREWS

ROCKET RESEARCH FACILITY

THE BEGINNING OF THE RACE

The United States and the Soviet Union both realized exactly how significant rocket research would become for the military after World War II. Each enlisted the best German rocket scientists for assistance with their research. Both sides soon were making progress with rocket technology.

The Race started in 1955 as both countries broadcast they soon would be launching their satellites. The Soviets felt that this announcement was a challenge and went as far as establishing a commission to beat the US in sending a satellite into space.

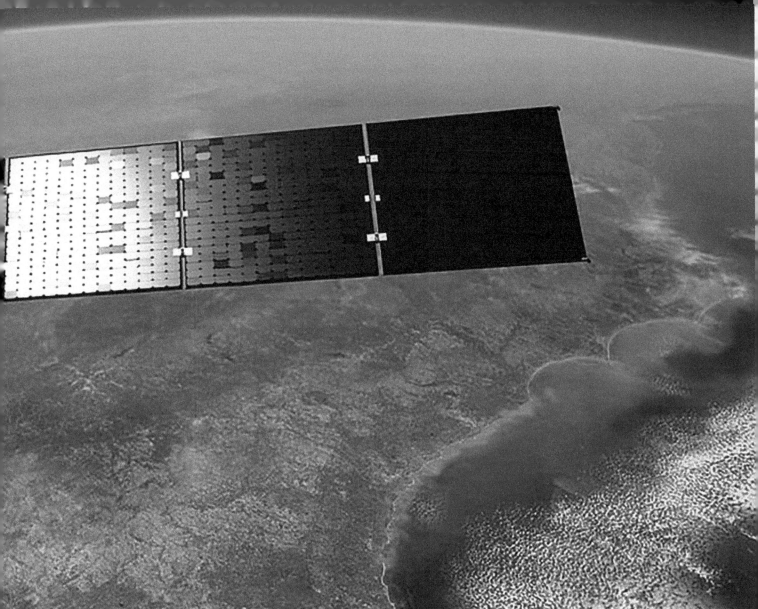

SATELLITE

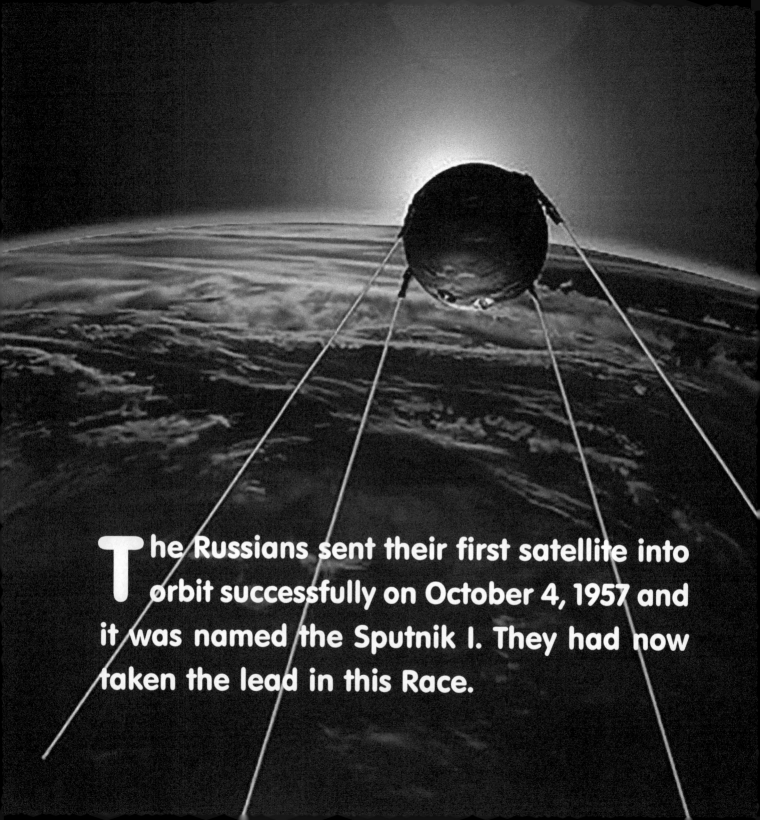

The Russians sent their first satellite into orbit successfully on October 4, 1957 and it was named the Sputnik I. They had now taken the lead in this Race.

The Americans then launched their first satellite successfully four months later, named the Explorer I.

THE FIRST MAN IN ORBIT

Again, the Soviets won by putting the first man in space on April 12, 1961. It was a man known as   and he was the first to orbit the Earth in the Russian spacecraft named Vostok I.

YURI GAGARIN

ALAN SHEPHERD

The US launched Freedom 7 three weeks later and became the first American astronaut in space. However, his spacecraft did not orbit Earth. On February 20, 1962, almost a year later, John Glenn was the first American to orbit the Earth aboard the Friendship 7 spacecraft.

RACING TO THE MOON

Being behind in the Space Race was embarrassing to the Americans. In 1961, President Kennedy addressed congress advising that he wished to be first to get a man on the moon. He believed it was important for our country as well as the western world. This was the beginning of the Apollo Moon program.

PRESIDENT JOHN F. KENNEDY

NASA-S-65-893

GEMINI SPACECRAFT

THE GEMINI PROGRAM

A long with the Apollo program, the US also launched the Gemini program to develop technology to use aboard the Apollo spacecraft. With the Gemini program, Americans were able to learn how to change the spacecraft's orbit, they spent a great amount of time in orbit so they could learn how it would affect the human body, they learned about bringing two craft together while in space, as well as going on the first walks outside of a craft.

MAN ON THE MOON

After several years of test flights, experiments, as well as training, the Apollo 11 was launched on July 16, 1969. The crew consisted of astronauts Neil Armstrong, Michael Collins, and Buzz Aldrin. It took three days to reach the moon.

NEIL ARMSTRONG, MICHAEL COLLINS AND BUZZ ALDRIN

Upon arrival, Armstrong and Aldrin moved to the Lunar module, named the Eagle, and started their descent to the moon. They encountered some malfunctions and Armstrong had to manually land the module.

The Eagle proceeded to land on July 20, 1969. It was then that Neil Armstrong stepped outside, became the first man to walk on the Moon, and with his first step, he proclaimed "That's one small step for man, one giant leap for mankind".

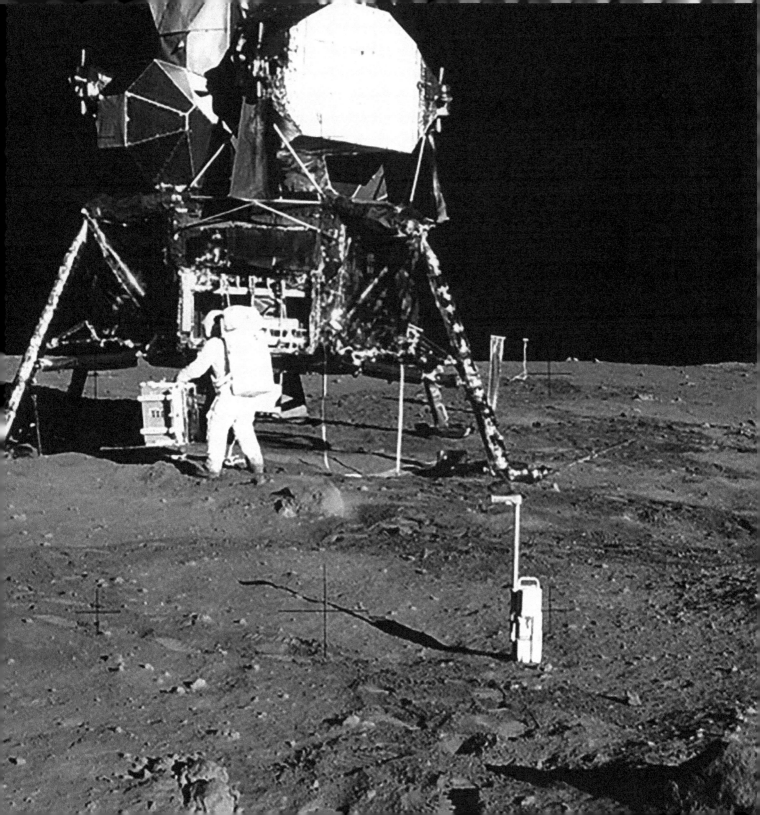

APOLLO-SOYUZ TEST PROJECT
SYMBOLIC PAINTING

THE END OF THE RACE

The United States now had taken a tremendous lead with the Gemini and Apollo programs. With the relationship between the Soviet Union and the United States starting to thaw, in July of 1975 the first US-Soviet joint mission took place with the Apollo-Soyez project. The Space Race was now effectively over.

ASTRONAUTS

An astronaut is someone specifically trained for outer space travel. Each astronaut aboard a craft might have varying responsibilities. There is typically a commander that leads the mission, as well as a pilot. Some of the other positions include a mission specialist, a flight engineer, a science pilot, and a payload commander.

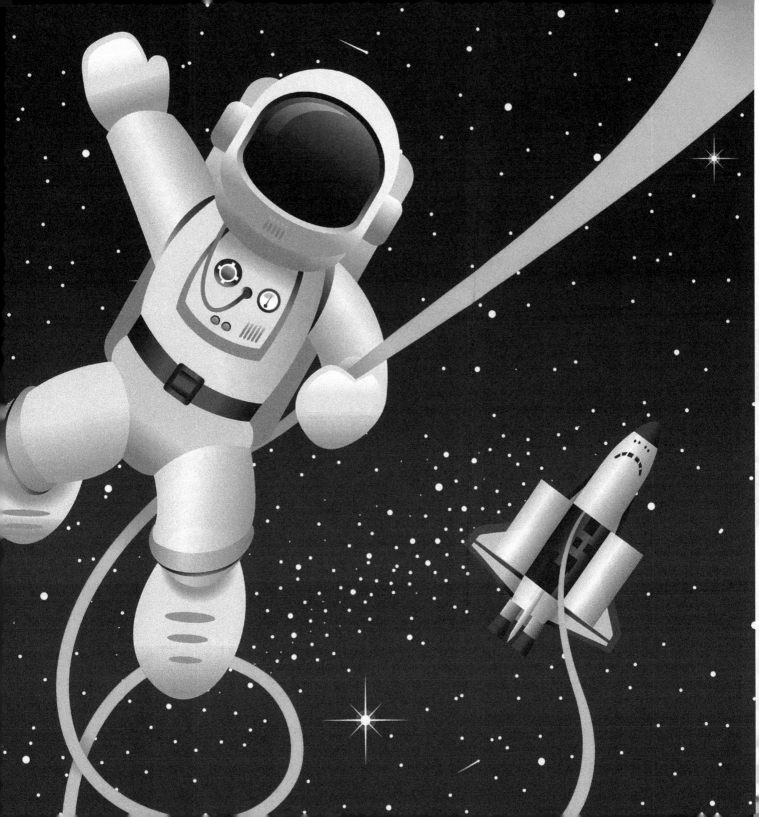

NASA NEUTRAL BUOYANCY
LABORATORY ASTRONAUT TRAINING

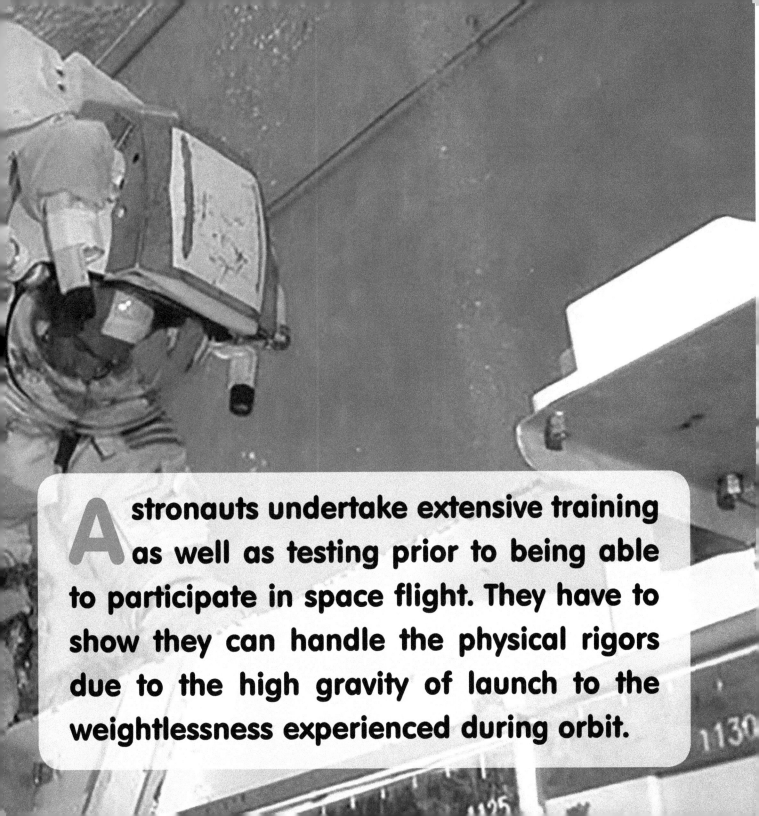

Astronauts undertake extensive training as well as testing prior to being able to participate in space flight. They have to show they can handle the physical rigors due to the high gravity of launch to the weightlessness experienced during orbit.

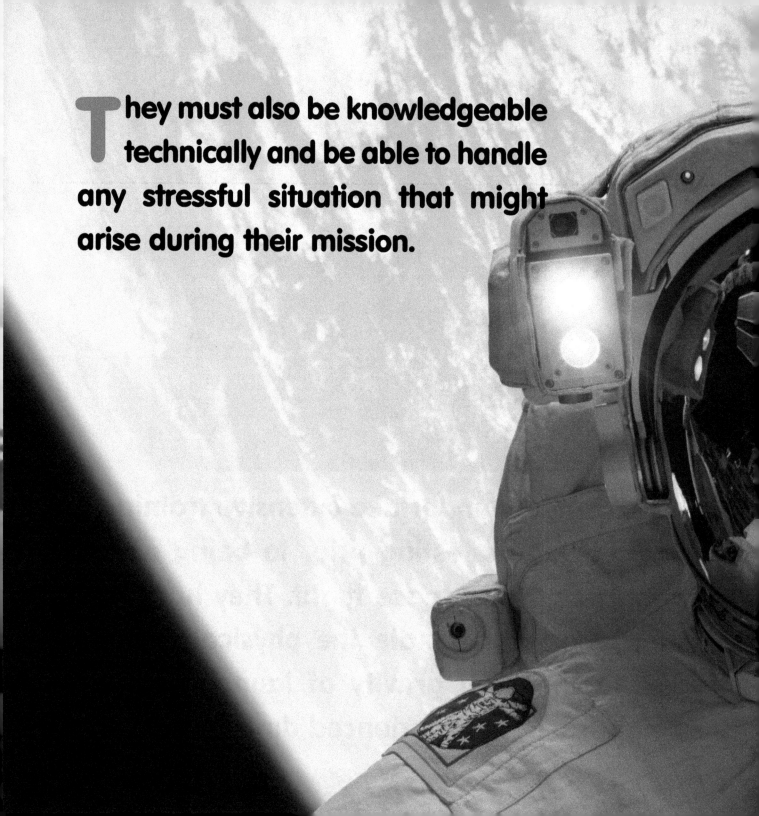

They must also be knowledgeable technically and be able to handle any stressful situation that might arise during their mission.

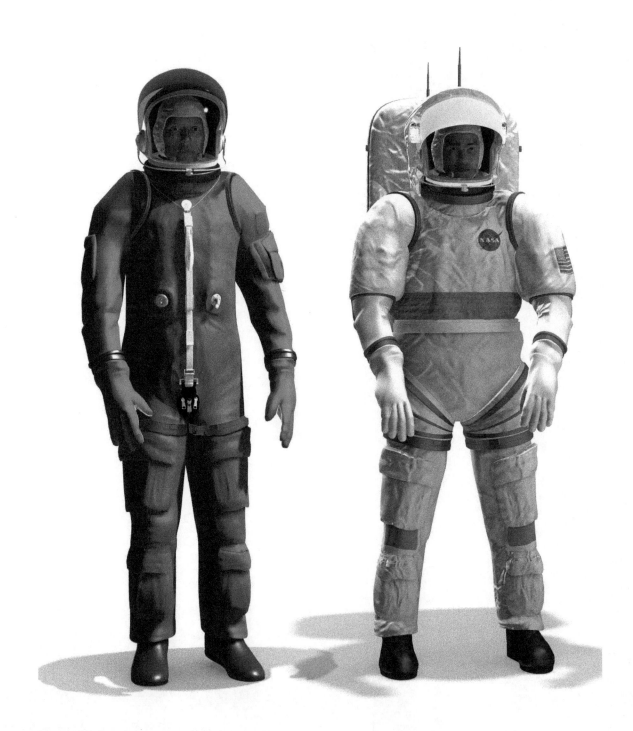

THE SPACESUITS

The spacesuit is special gear that an astronaut has to use when they are leaving the spacecraft. They provide air, they protect them from extreme temperatures in space, and they protect them from the sun's radiation.

Occasionally, the suits are tethered to the craft so that the astronaut will not float away.

O ther times, the suit might be equipped with small rocket thrusters allowing the astronaut the ability to navigate around the craft.

FAMOUS ASTRONAUTS

Other famous astronauts include Guion Bluford, Gus Grissom, John Glenn, Mae Jemison, Sally Ride and Valentina Tereshkova.This was such an exciting time for the United States. Being the first to walk on the moon was a major accomplishment after being so far behind during the Space War.

GUION BLUFORD

GUS GRISSOM

SALLY RIDE

JOHN GLENN

MAE JEMISON

VALENTINA TERESHKOVA

For additional information about Neil Armstrong and to learn about the other famous astronauts, you can go to your local library, research the internet, and ask questions of your teachers, family and friends.

Visit

BABY PROFESSOR
EDUCATION KIDS

www.BabyProfessorBooks.com

to download Free Baby Professor eBooks
and view our catalog of new and exciting
Children's Books

CPSIA information can be obtained
at www.ICGtesting.com
Printed in the USA
LVHW051544161222
735289LV00008B/1374